GUIDANCE

Biblical Direction For Life's Choices

Guidance - Biblical Direction For Life's Choices

Cover photo: Noel Davidson

Printed and Published by
AMBASSADOR PRODUCTIONS LTD.,
Providence House,
16 Hillview Avenue,
Belfast, BT5 6JR
U.K.

ISBN 1 898787 01 8

INTRODUCTION

A survey was conducted recently in decision-making and the study concluded that all of us face between 300 and 17,000 decisions every day! It is a very good thing in life to get into the habit of making decisions and acting on them for it is better to be right 50% of the time and get something done than it is to get nothing done because you are afraid to be wrong! Ronald Regan tells the story of how he learned the need for decision- making, early in life. An aunt had taken him to a cobbler to have a pair of shoes made for him. "Do you want a square toe or a round toe?", asked the cobbler. Regan hummed and hawed. So the cobbler said, "Come back in a day or two and let me know what you want". A few days later the shoemaker saw Regan on the street and asked what he had decided about the shoes. "I still haven't made up my mind", the boy answered. "Very well", said the cobbler. When Regan received the shoes, he was shocked to see that one shoe had a square toe and the other had a round toe! "Looking at those shoes every day taught me a lesson", said Regan, years later. "If you don't make your own decisions, somebody else will make them for you".

Guidance, from a Biblical stand-point, is all about making good decisions. This study aims to be Scriptural, not philosophical. It will aim at a practical exposition of Divine guidance in individual human life as taught in Scripture and proved in human experience. We will see that every detail of our lives, down to the very smallest, is to God, a necessary part of a magnificent whole. We will see that the shining mystery and rich reality of Biblical teaching for each individual believer is the reality of "The Father above me; controlling all things. The Saviour beside me; directing my footsteps. The Spirit within me, impressing me inwardly". The categorical truth of Scripture is that God does still guide His people. Some decisions in our lives are small ones and some are large, but God has promised to guide and help us to make those decisions as we pass through life's labyrinth of ways. He knows the future and He alone can give us that guidance for today which safeguards tomorrow. God has a purpose for each one of us as no-one else has. This study looks at the ways He guides and leads us to know and fulfil that purpose.

1. THE THREE LIGHTS

Many years ago a famous Christian writer was travelling from an Irish port to Holyhead on the Welsh coast. He was standing on the bridge with the captain, chatting to him about the voyage. "How do you know when you are on course for Holyhead?", he asked him. "When I approach the port", replied the captain, "I see three lights on the horizon. When I manoeuvre my ship to a position where I can make the three lights, one light, I am on course for Holyhead". The Christian writer lifted his pen when he got home and wrote of how Christians have three lights which are always on the horizon of their lives to guide them. When they find those three lights are one light, they can be sure they are on course for making a good decision in their lives within the will of God. The first light is the light of the Scriptures. If the Scriptures are against what you are going to do, then don't do it. They have spoken out clearly on a multitude of issues from marriage to communication, from neighbourhood relations to handling enemies, from running a business to life's true priorities, from being a good parent to finding the way to Heaven. If the Scriptures have spoken clearly and directly on an issue, then we need no further guidance on the issue; we simply obey the Scriptures.

There are, of course, other things on which the Scriptures have not spoken clearly. They have not told us, for example, whether to go to Portavogie or Portugal for our holidays, have they? They have not told us whether to wear blue socks or red socks, today. They have not told us which specific person to marry or not to marry. They have not spelled out which particular house to buy or not to buy, which particular flat to rent or which college or university to study in, or what particular job to take or refuse. In such situations, God uses another light on the horizon of the believer's life, the light of circumstance. Suddenly we find ourselves in a particular circumstance and wonder what on earth is going on. Our very lives at times may seem to be caving in and it almost appears as if God has forgotten us. Do you not think Joseph wondered what God was up to when his brothers threw him in a pit? Do you think, had you been talking to him, he would have said, "It's wonderful down here, I am on my way to becoming Prime Minister of Egypt?". Do you think as his brothers sold him to the Ishmaelites who took him as a slave to Egypt that he had any idea that the day would come when Pharoah would say to Joseph, "Without your consent no man may lift his hand or foot in all the land of Egypt"?

As Joseph entered into prison because a very evil woman had lied about him, he did not know that the prison was God's highway to the palace! Circumstances in our lives are often dark, but, if we only realised it, they are God's light in the path of guidance to lead us on to the next important phase of our lives. The Scripture tells us that "On the first day of the week Mary Magdalene came to the tomb early, while it was still dark". She found the Saviour's tomb, empty, and thought it was the darkest day of her life. Frantically she went searching for His body, telling Peter in despair of what had happened. She even found what she thought was the gardener and said, "Sir, if you have carried Him away, tell me where you have laid Him and I will come and take Him away". Superbly, of course, what Mary thought was the darkest day of her life turned out to be the best day of her life. In fact, it turned out to be the best day in the history of the entire world. The supposed gardener turned out to be the risen Christ! The greatest news the world every heard came out of a graveyard!

Don't, then, panic when circumstances seem to threaten. God uses circumstances as a light to guide you. Yet, on their own, circumstances as a guide can be dangerous. Jonah, the rebellious prophet, found his circumstances very conducive. The wind was in the right direction. The ship's captain was amiable. Jonah had money in his pocket. He said, in effect, "Viva, Espania!" and set sail for the Spanish coast. Circumstances looked fine but the Word of the Lord had already told Jonah to go to Nineveh. It took very frightening circumstances to arise in order to bring Jonah to see that when God guides us, the light of circumstances and the light of His Word must be one before we set sail on a new phase of our lives. The third light is the light of the "Peace of God". There is a great difference between "Peace with God" and the "Peace of God". When a person receives Christ as Saviour, they are justified by faith and immediately have "Peace with God through our Lord Jesus Christ". That means they are no longer at enmity with God, they are now at peace with Him. All hell cannot remove a person from that position. "The Peace of God", though, is different. It is conditional. "In everything, by prayer and supplication with thanksgiving, let your requests be made known to God and the peace of God which surpasses all understanding will guard your hearts and minds through Christ Jesus", says the Bible.

When Christians request something from God with a thankful heart for what God has already given them, then the "Peace of God", the tranquillity of God's own eternal being, the peace which God Himself has, the calm serenity that characterises His very nature, will become theirs. Yet, we must always remember, it is conditional. It comes by prayer and an attitude of thankfulness. God's peace is able to produce better results than human planning and is more effective for removing anxiety than any intellectual effort or power of reasoning. It "rises above every mind". It will protect the Christian's heart and mind, i.e. the Christian's entire inner being; emotions, affections, thoughts, and, vitally important, all their moral choices. This is what Christians mean when they say, "Do you have peace about it?". They mean does a sense of the peace of God fill your mind and heart about what you are going to decide to do in a given circumstance. Even if the whole world is shoving you to do something, if you do not have a sense of the peace of God about what you are going to do, don't let them budge you.

So it is that when faced with a decision in life, a Christian must make sure that the light of the Word of God, the light of circumstance, and the light of the peace of God, are one light. If one of these three is missing, wait until it comes into line and then proceed. You will find that God's lights of guidance, if followed, will never lead you on to the rocks. Trust Him.

2. ARE YOU UP-TIGHT ABOUT GUIDANCE?

Despite the lights of guidance that God provides along the voyage of life, a lot of people are very up-tight about knowing God's will in their lives. In fact many are full of fear and guilt on the subject. Why? It all stems from the fact that they think they have missed the will of God for their lives. You know the type; "God called me to go up the Amazon as a missionary when I was twenty-two but I didn't go and now the rest of my Christian life is a failure". There is another fear many Christians experience. It is not that they have deliberately disobeyed God's call, it is that they fear they have, unintentionally, misread it. They fear they have an innate lack of ability to read God's signs of guidance correctly. J.I. Packer puts it very well when he likens our fears about guidance to thinking that God's plan for our lives is like an itinerary drawn up by a travel agent. As long as we follow the agent's instructions and be in the right place, at the right time, boarding each aircraft, bus or boat as indicated, then all is well. But miss one of the pre-planned connections and the itinerary is ruined.

A revised plan can only be second-best compared with the original programme. Is this your view of God's will for your life? Is this your view of God? If you miss a connection here or there along the way, do you really think God cannot bring you back to His purpose for you? Have you forfeited your usefulness? Let me ask if you would treat your own child in such a manner? I doubt it very much. Why then do you think your Heavenly Father, who is love itself, would treat you, His child, differently? Let's look at some characters in Scripture who made a mess of things regarding the will of God in their lives. It is a fascinating meditation. Take Abraham, for an example. Abraham panicked on the path of God's will and fled to Egypt, lying to Pharoah that Sarah his wife was his sister to protect himself. God had given Abraham great promises that He would guide and direct him but he forgot about those promises and lived on his wits. He was thrown out of Egypt by Pharoah. What hope would you have given that Abraham would become a legend and an inspiration in history, as a man of staggering faith in God? None! Yet, he did become just that. God got him back on track and he became known as the Father of the Faithful.

Think about Moses. A meditation on the life of Moses, after murdering an Egyptian in order, he thought, to further God's cause will not lead you to the conclusion that God made sure he became a second rate leader because of his disastrous mistake. He became one of the greatest leaders in all of history.

What do you make of the con-man Jacob? Manipulative, supplanting, self-centred Jacob made sure, by foul means, that things went his way. Look at what God did through him; he became a "Prince" with God. His disastrous beginning did not ensure a disastrous end.

Could we have a greater example in all of Scripture of a person who, despite much error, eventually fulfilled the will of God for his life than Samson? Quite frankly, Samson disobeyed virtually every rule in God's book. Yet, the angel told his mother that he would "Begin to deliver Israel from the Philistines". Did he?

What is your view of Samson? A big lout? A he-man with a she- weakness? A man who fooled about with God's gifts to him and who was eventually discarded by God? This is not God's ultimate view. He certainly did deliberately disobey God's instructions to him on many occasions but for many years I reckon about twenty) he judged Israel successfully. His failures are highlighted by God for our learning, but, when Samson died, he effected a greater deliverance from the enemies of God's people by his death than even by his life!

There was no doubt that the enemies of God eventually knew where Samson's strength originated. He got back on track, all right, with a vengeance!

Did Peter not disobey God's will for his life? Most certainly. He denied to a teenage girl that he even knew the Christ. He who had said he would die for the Saviour miserably failed to live for Him on the night when the Saviour needed him most. Was he thrown aside by the Lord? Did be become a God's second-best Christian?

Have you read any of Peter's New Testament letters recently? There are fewer passages of Scripture more inspiring for people going through trouble. Was he restored to God's purpose for his life? Fewer have known a more complete restoration. A few weeks later he was leading thousands to faith in Christ. The Saviour met Peter by the lake, warmed him by a fire and fed him with fish and pointed him to the way back. Peter discovered that neither his sin, nor his temper or mood, nor the passage of time had lessened Christ's love for him nor dampened Christ's desire to see Peter live out God's purposes for his life.

So, Christian, if you have made a bad decision or sinned in disobeying God's clear instructions to you, it is categorically not the end. God knew that you and I were failures before He took us on. He has promised never to leave us nor forsake us, no matter who else does. As He told the erring Abraham, "I am your shield and your exceeding great reward". God loves us and is not going to put us on the scrap-heap or the shelf just because we have erred. It is true that sin has its earthly consequences and that stupid and silly decisions have repercussions but if there is repentance on our part and a willingness to try again, God can restore and use us.

Let me sign out this chapter with a more modern example of what we are thinking about. A wild, dissolute and drunken youth went one evening to a home Bible study amongst a few Christians in Germany. He got converted to Christ. Fervent in his faith but pretty empty in Scriptural knowledge he thought that God wanted him to be a missionary. Having a knowledge of betting on horses he went to a racecourse and put a bet on a horse. "If it wins, Lord", he prayed, "I will know you want me to be a missionary!". If you had been passing that racecourse you wouldn't have given much hope for that young man ever finding God's will in his life, would you?

His name was George Muller and he became one of the greatest Christians in British history! Selah.

So, quit being up-tight about guidance. Admit your mistakes, repent if you have been disobedient and sinful and trust in the Lord with all your heart, lean not to your own understanding, in all your ways acknowledge Him and He shall direct your paths.

3. OBEYING STANDING ORDERS

A lot of people think of Divine guidance in terms of special Divine intervention in the life of a Christian every time he or she has a major decision to make. Is such a view scriptural? Does God intervene every time we have to make decisions?

Let's take it on the human level, first. Parents in training children do not intervene in every decision their children make in life, do they? Certainly not. Why? Because if they did, their children would never grow up. They would never learn to make responsible decisions later in life if they were not given freedom to make some earlier in life. A parent intervening all the time would create a very spoiled child bereft of social skills needed for balanced living. Such an approach would also create a child who would be eventually seriously flawed in any decision-making process in their life.

What would any wise parent do in order to aid their child to be a good decision-maker? They would set their child limits to observe. Obviously a child would not be allowed to do whatever it wanted because, out of lack of experience for a start, it might choose a line of action whose consequences the child would simply not be capable of knowing. To allow it complete freedom would bring incalculable disaster. Yet, drawing from the wisdom of his parents and their example, and observing the limits set, a child can be allowed freedom to make decisions.

By such a process the child slowly but surely grows up to be a responsible adult.

Let's take these guidelines to the spiritual level. God wants His children to grow up responsibly. He wants them to be able to use their minds and exercise their spiritual muscles and make good decisions in their lives. Though, He too sets limits to observe. The Bible shows very clearly what God hates to see in His image-bearers. So we, by His grace, can avoid those things that God hates. Drawing, then, from God's wisdom and observing the limits He sets as revealed in the Scriptures and having His example to follow as reflected in the life of the Lord Jesus while He was here on earth, we are allowed to use our minds to make good decisions and so grow up as responsible Christians.

There is, in Scripture, a very gripping and instructive example of those principles we have just been thinking about. It concerns a very important pivot in the history of the Christian church, namely, the story of how Paul was guided to first bring the Gospel of Jesus Christ to Europe.

Consider the scene. God wants to bring Paul to Europe to sow a very important seed whose harvest we are enjoying today. Did He intervene in Paul's life with a flash of lightning from the sky or have some Scripture verse burden him heavily to shift him from the Middle East to Europe? Not on this occasion.

We simply read in Acts 15; 36 that "After some days Paul said to Barnabas, "'Let us now go back and visit our brethren in every city where we have preached the Word of the Lord and see how they are doing"'.

What were Paul and Barnabas doing? They were simply responding to God's standing order that shepherds of God's flock should care for and feed their sheep. Paul and Barnabas needed no special guidance for that any more than Germans need a letter from their Chancellor, or the British need a letter from their Queen or Americans need a letter from their President every week to tell them to pay their taxes! As a friend of mine once put it, "What mother, in normal circumstances, would earnestly pray to the Lord for direct special guidance whether it was His will that she give her baby its breakfast?"

The plain fact is that we don't need special Divine guidance in a whole lot of areas of activity in our lives. The standing order to the Christian is to be a good citizen, a good neighbour, to spread the Gospel, to care for family and friends, etc. So, let's get on with the standing orders, just like Paul did and if we need special intervention from God to guide us, we will get it. Paul did. As he went to encourage the churches he had planted, God intervened with special guidance, twice. Yet, notice that it was with negative intervention, telling him not to go to Asia or Bithynia. (See Acts 16; 6-7).

It is vital to understand that all of this time Paul and those friends with him were never given advance information as to where God was eventually leading them! Paul didn't know that when God stopped him going to preach in Asia and then in Bithynia that the whole purpose was to get him to go to Philippi. Moses' parents didn't get advance information that when they put their baby in an ark of bulrushes and floated it in the Nile, that Pharoah's daughter would find the child, adopt him and that God would get Moses to eventually lead the Children of Israel across the wilderness! You don't get advance information from God that when you lose a job, or are passed over for promotion, or are sidelined by your friends through no fault of your own, that it will all lead to a wonderful goal God has for you in the future. Everything that happens to us is not necessarily good, but it always works together for good.

Special Divine guidance may not necessarily let you know where you are being led. It may be just to keep you "On track" on the line of obeying God's standing orders.

Eventually Paul and his friends arrived in Troas. We are not told how long it took them to get there but it must have been a very long journey taking up a considerable amount of time. They got special Divine guidance in the form of a vision which Paul had in the night. A man from Macedonia stood and pleaded with Paul saying, "Come over to Macdonia and help us".

Did Paul jump out of bed in the morning and say, "Right men, we are off to Europe?". He did not. He first of all talked over what he had experienced with his friends and the Scripture says that they "concluded" (i.e. inferred) that the Lord had called them to Macedonia. It is, therefore, a very good idea to discuss with Godly and caring friends those things which you consider to be special Divine guidance in your life.

Paul and his party eventually arrived in Philippi and the Lord opened Lydia's heart to the Gospel. She in turn opened her home to Paul and Silas and God in turn opened the continent of Europe to the best news it ever heard.

What do we learn, then, from this Scriptural story to help us in the nitty gritty of seeking God's guidance for our daily lives? If we were never allowed to decide anything but were always controlled by constant interventions from God directly guiding us, we would never grow up to be mature Christians.

When God's plans or our needs require it, God can and often does intervene with special guidance. This may be in the form of a dramatic intervention or may be through a circumstance such as bumping into a friend, receiving a telephone call, reading a magazine article or crossing a certain street. Great doors swing on little hinges.

God sets limits for our behaviour by showing us in the Bible the things that He hates. If we, by His grace, avoid these, our decisions within these limits will bring glory to Him and help us to mature. God never by-passes or suppresses our moral or spiritual judgment. If God broke your mind, you would be as a jelly-fish or a vegetable. He helps you by His Holy Spirit to will to do His will. When a good door closes, God opens a better one.

4. WHEN IS THE WRONG ROAD THE RIGHT ROAD?

Question: When is the wrong road, the right road?
Answer: When God sends you on it.

Here are some stories to illustrate this truth.

Some years ago, the late Bishop Taylor Smyth was travelling by railway from somewhere in northern England to somewhere south. He missed a connection at

Leeds, Yorkshire, and found he had two hours to wait. As always, in such circumstances, he accepted this as "permissive Providence", and prayed for guidance, asking if God had some special purpose in allowing the delay. Strolling from the station to the big square outside, he sat on a form, and noticed that its only other occupant was a middle-aged man who looked the very picture of misery. Shabbily dressed, bent shoulders, head drooped down on his hands, he took no notice whatever of the burly clergyman who now sat near him. Still counting on guidance, the Bishop said, "You seem to be in some deep trouble". "Yes, I sure am", the man muttered, without lifting his eyes. "I'm at the end of things, Mr". He coughed hoarsely, then added, "Maybe you'll not believe me, Mr, but tonight I'm going to end everything; and I'm just having this last sit out here". "But is there no-one can help you?", asked the Bishop. "Nobody", came the dejected reply.

After a pause, head sagging still lower, the man added, "Begging your pardon, stranger, there's just one man who could have helped me, if I could have found him; but I haven't seen him these fifteen years, and I have no notion where he is". "Who is he?" asked the Bishop.

"He was my army Padre in France during the war, but I clean forget his name". "Which regiment and company were you in? What battles were you in?", enquired the Bishop. The man slowly told him, still without looking up. Then, stretching out his hand, and gently lifting the man's head up, the Bishop said, "Well, my brother, look at me; your man is right here; I was that Padre; and after all these years God has sent me to help you here and now!".

Just recently a friend of mine, a mathematics lecturer at a Welsh University, missed his train connection in a European city. His colleagues were greatly perturbed by the incident but my friend contented himself with the fact that God makes no mistakes. He waited for another connection and eventually settled down in his railway carriage. There he got into conversation with a couple from, of all places, Siberia. He discovered them to be vitally interested in spiritual things and happening to have a Russian Bible in his case, offered it to them.

Their surprise was quite overwhelming. How could he know that just a few weeks previously they had had their most precious possession stolen; namely, their Bible. The woman hugged her new-found copy as if it were the crown jewels!

My friend knew, then, why he had missed his connection.

Would anybody stubbornly pretend that such happenings are mere coincidences? Surely they are the operation of real Divine guidance in and through consecrated individuals. What channels of blessing we might become if we were only living such guided lives! Don't think, though, that leading such a guided life brings wonderful consequences immediately. I love to tell the story of my good friends at Capernwray Hall, the Christian Conference Centre and Bible School situated in its own beautiful grounds in Lancashire, England. A while back the directors of Capernwray Hall bought a castle in Austria as a holiday and conference centre and God richly blessed them in their work there. They wondered why things were so especially blessed until one day they found a Bible belonging to the man who had built the castle. He had written a prayer on the fly- leaf of the Bible asking God to use the castle to His glory. Though the man had done his best to serve the Lord, holding services in the castle, and witnessing to others, he was severely persecuted throughout his Christian life. He died, heartbroken and with no evident results from his faithful service. He seemed to have been on the wrong road of service. Was he? Not at all. God answered his prayer when my friends from Capernwray moved in. The significant thing, though, is that my friends discovered the Bible and its written prayer to be seven hundred years old!

Are you discouraged on the path of doing what you know to be the will of God? Have you had clear guidance and have sought all these months, and maybe even years, to do it? Is there no great sign that you are being successful? Who said that you were to be judged on outward success, encouraging as it is when it comes? Surely what you are called to be is to be faithful. In the end, doing God's will is good, perfect and acceptable, though, at the time you are carrying it out, it appears to be anything but scintillating.

Take Amy Carmichael, the great Christian Missionary to India. Amy set up a superb work in South India to rescue little children from being sold into temple prostitution. Hundreds were saved from this dreadful trade and, yet, one night Amy fell into a hole unlit by builders in her compound and became an invalid for thirty years. From that invalid's bed came some of the most moving and Christ-exalting Christian literature ever written, which has in turn touched millions of lives. In Switzerland, recently, to preach God's Word I came across an older Christian lady who had worked with Amy all those years ago and as we talked around her dining room table, she told me how the invalided Amy used to keep a lamp burning in her window at night. "That lamp is for you", she said, "To cheer you as you return to your bungalow from your day's labour for the Lord Jesus".

What seemed to be a devastatingly "wrong road" turned out in the over- ruling providence of God to be a road of incredible blessing. Recently a member of my Bible Class and an outstanding Christian student leader called Kirsty Noble sent me the following poem. The author is unknown but the poem is powerfully relevant to the theme we have just been talking about it. I ask you to ponder these words very carefully.

She asked to be made like her Saviour,
And He took her at her word,
And sent her a heart-crushing burden
Till the depths of her soul were stirred.
She asked for a faith strong, yet simple.
He permitted the dark clouds to come;
She staggered by faith through the darkness,
As the storms did her soul o'erwhelm.

She prayed to be filled with a passion
Of love for lost souls and for God,
And again in response to her longing,
She sank 'neath the chastening rod.
She wanted a place in His vineyard;
He took her away from her home,
And placed her among hardened sinners

Where she humanly stood all alone.
She gave up all worldly ambitions,
Those "castles in air" of years.
And she knelt in deep consecration,
And whispered "Amen" through her tears.
She wanted a meek, lowly spirit -
The work He gave answered that cry;
And those who had been her companions
With pitying smile passed her by.

She asked to lean hard on her Saviour;
He took human props quite away,
Till no earthly friend could help her,
And she could do nothing but pray.
I saw her go out to the vineyard
To harvest the golden grain;
Her eyes were still moistened with weeping,
Her heart was still throbbing with pain.

But many a heart that was broken,
And many a wrecked, blighted life
Was made to thank God for her coming,
And rejoice in the midst of the strife.
She had prayed to be made like her Saviour,
And the burden He gave her to bear
Had been but the great Sculptures training;
Thus answering her earnest prayer.

5. THE ROLE OF THE BIBLE IN GUIDANCE

It constantly amazes me how few people actually read the Scriptures. In The Dark Ages, copies of the Scriptures were chained to the pulpit in the secret language of the clergy and the public were kept stone ignorant of the life-changing teaching of its truths. Men like Tyndale were then burnt alive for trying to get the Scriptures into the hands of the common people. In those days Biblical ignorance was forced. Now, in our day, it is voluntary. In fact the more versions of Scripture we have, the less the Bible is read. What I have just written, though, needs to be qualified. We need to remember that more than half the languages of the world have no portion of Scripture at all. This embraces, perhaps, one hundred and fifty million people. In many areas there are very severe restrictions on the publication and sale of the Bible. The sad fact remains, though, particularly in the western world, that when people have the Scriptures in their own language with a ready access to them and absolute freedom to study them, so few actually do in comparison with those who don't!

In a school, here in the West, a teacher quizzed a group of college-bound High School pupils on the Bible. Here are some of the answers he received;

> Jesus was baptized by Moses.
> Sodom and Gomorrah were lovers.
> Jezel was Ahab's donkey.
> The New Testament Gospels were written by Matthew, Mark, Luther and John.
> Eve was created from an apple.
> The most hilarious, if sad, answer to the question,
> "What was Golgotha?" was,
> "Golgotha was the name of the giant who slew the Apostle David".

Despite the fact that millions neglect the Scriptures, it does not take away the reality that there is no other place where better guidance can be found for everyday living. Just recently I talked with one of my local church's elders who was off to Kiev to teach business ethics to businessmen emerging from Communism. His textbook was the book of Proverbs!

To move away from the pages of Scripture is to enter into the waste-lands of subjectivity. The Bible is a divinely provided map containing directions and markings to guide people to the true order for family or nation. To ignore its teachings leads to moral and spiritual shipwreck. I am calling, in this little booklet, for a return to actually reading, for at least twenty minutes each day, a portion of Scripture. No, I don't mean reading the Bible just to prepare a Sunday School class, or to prepare sermons or a talk at the local prison chapel or old-folks' homes.

I mean reading the Bible for twenty minutes every day for yourself.

Get a "One Year Bible" which divides the Scripture up into readings which will take you from Genesis to Revelation in one year. (There is even a "One Minute Bible" which will give you one minute daily readings, but, I challenge you to twenty minutes a day!). No matter where you are, no matter who you have got to meet, no matter what deadlines crop up, spend twenty minutes in the Word every day. Right? There is of course nothing magical in reading the Scriptures. They need to be obeyed and you need to know the Author, which is possible through Jesus Christ. We know very well that professional religious types have been merely reading the Scriptures and disobeying them for centuries. Even the Pharisees of Christ's day who read the Bible constantly, put the Saviour they spoke of on a cross and then went right back to reading the Scriptures again. It is obviously important that the Scriptures are obeyed and the Saviour they present, trusted. Yet, if you read the Scriptures regularly, the benefits are enormous. If you doubt me, just check out these points from Psalm 119. They spell out the benefits very clearly;

1. God's Word establishes my way. (v.5)
2. God's Word purifies my life. (v.9-11)
3. God's Word gives me counsel. (v.24)
4. God's Word removes everything false in me. (v.29)
5. God's Word produces reverence for God. (v.38)
6. God's Word increases my courage. (v.46)
7. God's Word comforts me in afflictions. (v.50)
8. God's Word guards me from panic. (v.61-62)
9. God's Word teaches me discernment and knowledge. (v.65-66)
10. God's Word makes me resourceful. (v.79)
11. God's Word cultivates patience. (v.87)
12. God's Word keeps me spiritually recharged. (v.93)
13. God's Word accelerates my understanding. (v.98-100)
14. God's Word creates a joyful heart. (v.111)
15. God's Word sustains me when I feel helpless. (v.116)
16. God's Word enables me to honour what is right and hate what is wrong. (v.128)
17. God's Word causes me to walk in the truth. (v.133)

18. God's Word surrounds me with delight in spite of difficulty. (v.143)
19. God's Word develops the discipline of prayer. (v.147)
20. God's Word rescues me when I am defenceless. (v.152-154)
21. God's Word fills me with praise without and peace within. (v.164-165)
22. God's Word draws me back when I stray. (v.176)

It is a fact that nothing else will do for me what the Scriptures will. It is vital that we make place for them in our daily lives. As for helping us in your decision-making, which, we have discovered is the main thrust of guidance, there is a grid of some Biblical principles and some checkpoints which together constitute the way of wisdom for all who follow the Lord. These have been helpfully listed by J. I. Packer. So, then, when we have a decision to make, let us, remember;

1. THERE ARE INSTRUCTIONS TO HEED

There is obviously no point in asking God for guidance if we refuse to obey the instructions He has already given in the Scriptures. For example, the Scriptures say that "If I regard iniquity in my heart the Lord will not hear me". (Psalm 66; 18). This means that if I hug grudges, enjoy tittle-tattle, nurse jealousies, pass on gossip, lead an undisciplined, self-indulgent life, I disqualify myself from heart-to-heart fellowship with Christ and hold back guidance. If I obey the instructions in God's Word, I will find God's Will, if I disregard them, I won't.

Ninety per cent of knowing God's Will is, of course, being willing to do it before I even know what it is!

2. THERE ARE LIMITS TO OBSERVE

If I deliberately step beyond the limits God puts down in His Word for me, I will stray from His Will. The Lord Jesus said that the Christian walk would take us on what He described as a "narrow way." That narrow way does not get any wider the longer I am on it, does it? It will be narrow right to the end. There will be kerb-stones and fences, limits set to where I can walk. The "broad way", on the other hand, "which leads to destruction", has not got the same limits. On the broad way I can by and large say what I like, think what I like, behave how I like and, I can carry what baggage I like. The choice is mine. If I want to walk the narrow way which leads to life, I must observe the limits it sets.

3. THERE ARE EXAMPLES TO FOLLOW

There is nothing quite like Scripture to show me examples of men and women finding and doing God's Will in their lives. From the butler Nehemiah to the gleaner, Ruth; from the shepherd boy David to the fig- picker, Amos; from the intellectual Daniel to the little servant girl in the house of Naaman; from the garment-making Dorcas to the tent- making Paul, all found God's guidance and did His Will.

You and I can follow their example.

4. THERE IS WISDOM TO DRAW ON

I refer, in part, to the book of Proverbs. This book has a lot to say about the issues of life. Here is instruction for young people in a world where subtle and restless efforts are made to poison their hearts and pervert their ways. Here are verbal gold vaults of wisdom for parents raising a family. Here are words of advice for those who are unemployed and living from hand to mouth. Here is incisive warning about the power of speech. Here you will read wisdom regarding anger, education, food, drink, justice, greed, self- control, the place of a woman and the place of a man in society and much more.

To sum up our Biblical approach to guidance, here are ten checkpoints to help when we are seeking God's Will in any situation;

1. Ask the question; "What is the best I can do for my God in this situation?".
2. Note the instructions of Scripture; on many issues the Bible has already spoken.
3. Follow the examples of Godliness in Scripture. Imitate the love and humility of Jesus Himself.
4. Let wisdom judge the best course of action; the question we should ask is no longer; "What is God's Will?"; instead thequestion is; "How do I make good decisions?"

5. Always note nudges from God that come your way; special burdens of concern or restlessness of heart might indicate that something needs to be changed.
6. Cherish the Divine peace that Paul says, "garrisons" the hearts of those who are in God's Will.
7. Observe the limits set by circumstances to what is possible. When it is clear those limits cannot be changed, accept them as from God.
8. Be prepared for God's guidance to be withheld until the right time comes for a decision. God usually guides one step at a time.
9. Be prepared for God to direct you to something you do not like, and teach you to like it!
10. Never forget that if you make a bad decision, it is not the end. God forgives and restores.

Thank you so much for reading this booklet and it is our prayer that you may experience the joy of knowing God's Will in your life. Ninety per cent of knowing God's Will is, of course, being ready to do it even before He reveals it to you. Are you ready?

Oh, to be always ready,
To do Thy perfect Will;
Alert for every challenge
Thy purpose to fulfil!
Ready with fervent daring
In holy war for Thee;
Ready for burden-bearing
If that Thy Will should be.
Oh, to be always ready
To go or to obey,
A "vessel unto honour",
"Prepared" and "Sanctified"!
Ready for witness-bearing,
Though stumbling, truly wise,
Ready for sorrow-sharing,
To soothe and sympathise.
Oh, to be always ready,
To serve without applause,
Forgiving, calm and steady,
If blamed without a cause;
Ready by daily lingerings,
In Thine own Word and prayer;
Ready, at last for Heaven,
To meet and serve Thee there.

J. Sidlow Baxter

Other Pathway Booklets in this series include:-

- **WORRY** - A Biblical Answer to the King of all Addictions
- **SUFFERING** - A Biblical Perspective on Life's Greatest Puzzle
- **VALUES** - Things Worth Standing Up For
- **BACKSLIDING** - It's Causes and Cure

£1.75 each plus 25p postage and packing

Ambassador Productions Ltd
16 Hillview Avenue,
Belfast, BT5 6JR
United Kingdom